NATIONAL GEOGRAPHIC

READING EXPEDITIONS®

W9-AYG-076

STAND UP AND SPEAK OUT

A Road to Freedom

*The Kelly and Garner Families Along
the Underground Railroad*

By George Cappacio
Illustrated by Rodney Pate

Picture Credits
4 © Corbis; 5 Mapping Specialists, Ltd.; 53
© Louie Psihoyos/Corbis; 54 (top to bottom)
The Granger Collection, New York, © Corbis;
56 (top) © Corbis, (left to right) © Bettmann/
Corbis, National Portrait Gallery, Smithsonian
Institution/Art Resource, New York.

Produced through the worldwide resources
of the National Geographic Society, John M.
Fahey, Jr., President and Chief Executive
Officer; Gilbert M. Grosvenor, Chairman of
the Board; Nina D. Hoffman, Executive Vice
President and President, Books and Education
Publishing Group.

**Prepared by National Geographic
School Publishing**
Ericka Markman, Senior Vice President and
President, Children's Books and Education
Publishing Group; Steve Mico, Senior Vice
President, Publisher, Editorial Director; Francis
Downey, Executive Editor; Richard Easby,
Editorial Manager; Bea Jackson, Director of
Design; Cindy Olson, Art Director; Margaret
Sidlosky, Director of Illustrations; Matt
Wascavage, Manager of Publishing Services;
Lisa Pergolizzi, Sean Philpotts, Production
Managers, Ted Tucker, Production Specialist.

Manufacturing and Quality Control
Christopher A. Liedel, Chief Financial Officer;
Phillip L. Schlosser, Director; Clifton M. Brown,
Manager.

Editors
Barbara Seeber, Mary Anne Wengel

Book Development
Morrison BookWorks LLC

Book Design
Steven Curtis Design

Art Direction
Dan Banks, Project Design Company

Published by the National Geographic Society
1145 17th Street, N.W.
Washington, D.C. 20036-4688

ISBN: 0-7922-5870-3

2012 2013 2014 2015
   3 4 5 6 7 8 9 10 11 12 13 14 15

✺ Contents ✺

Introduction 4

The Characters 6

ACT I 9
Cambridge, Maryland, March 1857
Scene 1 *In the woods near Cambridge*
Scene 2 *Inside the Cambridge Quaker
Meeting House*

ACT II 21
Cambridge, Maryland, April 1857
Scene 1 *In the kitchen of the Kelly home*
Scene 2 *In front of the jail in town*
Scene 3 *In the living room of the Kelly home*
Scene 4 *Outside the Kelly barn*

ACT III 41
Cambridge, Maryland, May 1857
Scene 1 *Inside the Cambridge Quaker
Meeting House*
Scene 2 *Outside the Kelly home*
Scene 3 *A country road outside Cambridge*

Epilogue 52

The Facts Behind the Story 53

Read, Research, and Write. 55

Extend Your Reading 56

Slaves or Citizens?

In 1860, nearly four million African Americans were slaves in the United States. Most slaves worked on farms in the South. Slaves were not thought of as human beings. They were thought of as property. Children whose mothers were slaves became slaves too. Slaves could not leave their owner's land without permission. They were often punished very harshly. Not everyone in the United States supported slavery. Many thought slavery was wrong. Some people fought to abolish, or end, slavery. Other Americans believed that the economy in the South needed slavery. They thought slavery should continue. The fight over slavery would eventually divide the United States and cause the Civil War.

Fighting Slavery in America

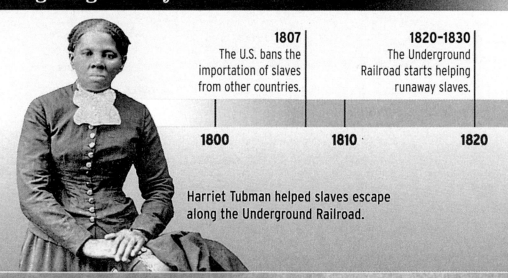

1807
The U.S. bans the importation of slaves from other countries.

1820-1830
The Underground Railroad starts helping runaway slaves.

1800   1810   1820

Harriet Tubman helped slaves escape along the Underground Railroad.

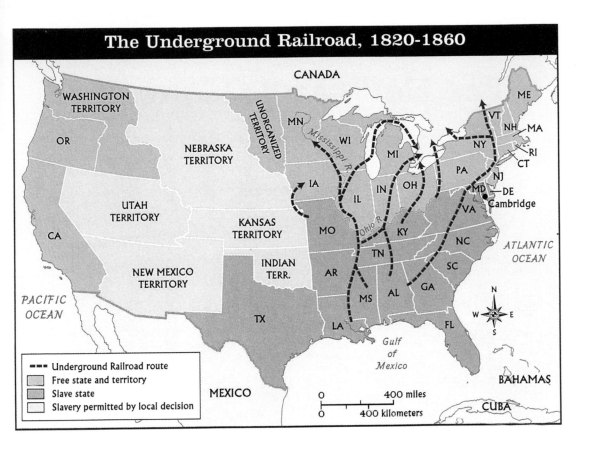

The Underground Railroad, 1820-1860

Legend:
- - - - Underground Railroad route
- Free state and territory
- Slave state
- Slavery permitted by local decision

0 ——— 400 miles
0 ——— 400 kilometers

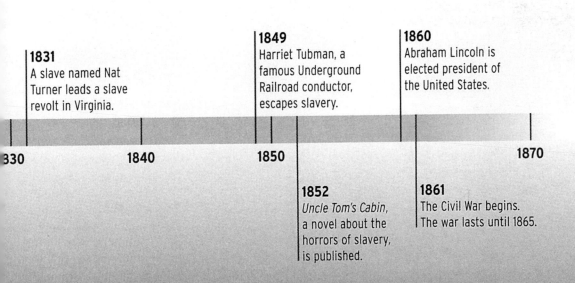

1831
A slave named Nat Turner leads a slave revolt in Virginia.

1849
Harriet Tubman, a famous Underground Railroad conductor, escapes slavery.

1860
Abraham Lincoln is elected president of the United States.

1830   1840   1850   1870

1852
Uncle Tom's Cabin, a novel about the horrors of slavery, is published.

1861
The Civil War begins. The war lasts until 1865.

The Kelly and Garner Families

Elias, Hannah, and James Kelly

The Kelly children all try to work against slavery. Elias, 17, wants to write for the newspaper. Hannah, 13, tutors free African Americans. James, 15, helps the family shelter runaway slaves.

John and Elizabeth Kelly

John is the father of the family, and Elizabeth is the mother. They are farmers and members of the Society of Friends. They are against slavery, and their house is a "station" along the Underground Railroad.

Ned Delaney

Ned is a farmer. He believes slavery should be allowed. He owns slaves. He regards abolitionists, like John Kelly, a threat to his way of life. Ned will do what he can to preserve his way of life.

Frances Garner

Frances is a runaway slave from Virginia. She has taken her two sons with her along the Underground Railroad. They have made it to Maryland, but she and her sons want to move farther north.

Lewis and Samuel Garner

Lewis, 10, and Samuel, 8, are eager to learn how to read. They become fond of Hannah Kelly, who reads her favorite stories to them.

Other Characters

Narrator
William Goodwin
Clerk of the Meeting
Martha Purvis
Sheriff Hollings
Quaker Man 1-3
Quaker Woman 1-3

Act I

The Setting

Cambridge, Maryland, March 1857

Scene 1

In the woods near Cambridge

Narrator: For several years, the Kelly family has opened their farmhouse to **fugitive** slaves escaping north on the Underground Railroad. This is very dangerous work. If the family is caught helping runaways, they might have to pay huge fines or go to jail. Worse yet, they could be beaten and killed by those who support slavery. But the Kellys believe they are doing the right thing. The example set by Harriet Tubman inspires them to go on with their work. Harriet was born a slave and raised in Dorchester County, Maryland. After her escape, she led more than 300 slaves to freedom on the Underground Railroad.

John Kelly never knows when new "passengers" will arrive. He must be ready at any time of the day or night. As Act I opens, John and his older son, Elias,

---

fugitive – a person who is running away

are secretly waiting in the woods for a family of fugitives. The muffled baying of bloodhounds can be heard in the distance. It's a frosty winter night. A light snow is falling.

Elias Kelly: *(Whispering)* See anything?

John Kelly: *(Looking around)* Not yet, but I'm sure he'll be here soon. I wish the moon wasn't so bright. I don't want anyone to see us.

Elias Kelly: I'm really cold. I hope he hurries up. Are you sure this is the right spot?

John Kelly: Of course. I've been meeting Goodwin here for years. It's the best place to land a boat on the river without being seen.

Elias Kelly: How many runaways do you think he'll bring?

John Kelly: I heard it's a family of three. A mother and her two boys.

Elias Kelly: From where?

John Kelly: From Southern Virginia, I believe. They will have already had a hard journey. They've had to travel across an entire state without anyone seeing them. And it is still so cold outside. They will need a good night's sleep.

Elias Kelly: And some luck, too. There are always plenty of slave catchers on the lookout.

John Kelly: Slave catchers do nothing more than make money from other people's misery. Will they ever recognize the pain they cause?

Elias Kelly: The sound of those dogs makes me shiver.

John Kelly: Sshh! You hear that?

Elias Kelly: What?

John Kelly: I don't know. Could be oars in the water, or maybe just waves slapping the shore. Listen.

Elias Kelly: I hear it, too. I hope those dogs don't get any closer.

John Kelly: I'm glad there's not much wind tonight. Hopefully they won't pick up our scent.

Elias Kelly: The sheriff would lock us both up if he knew what we are doing.

John Kelly: He would have to, since we are breaking the law.

Elias Kelly: It's an unjust law.

John Kelly: I agree that the law is unjust, but it is still the law. Sheriff Hollings would have every right to arrest us, so we must be careful. And I don't think our slave-holding neighbors would be too pleased to find out what we're up to.

Elias Kelly: Maybe our neighbors should work on treating people fairly instead of wasting time making enemies of us.

John Kelly: That's true, but for now all we can do is to continue helping slaves like these in whatever ways we can. If our neighbors find out what we're doing, they will stop us for sure.

Elias Kelly: Are those dogs getting closer? They sound vicious and they seem to be getting louder.

John Kelly: I hope not. If one of those slave catchers spots us, he'll shoot us on sight. I know their kind. All they care about is the reward money.

Elias Kelly: I think I see it.

John Kelly: What?

Elias Kelly: The boat, Goodwin's boat.

John Kelly: *(Squinting)* I see it, too. I can just make out the old man's face.

Elias Kelly: How long has he been a conductor?

John Kelly: Many years.

Elias Kelly: And he's never gotten caught?

John Kelly: No, but he takes a risk every time he chooses to cross that river.

Elias Kelly: *(Loudly)* William Goodwin, we're over here! Hey there! William Goodwin, we're over here behind the trees! This way—do you see us?

John Kelly: *(In a loud whisper)* For Pete's sake, Elias, be quiet! You want those hounds tearing after us? They can't be more than half a mile away now, maybe less. Let's go down to the river.

William Goodwin: *(Speaking softly)* John, is that you?

John Kelly: Yes. My son Elias is here, too.

William Goodwin: Give me a hand, son. I'm not as young as I once was.

(Elias helps William Goodwin climb out of his boat.)

John Kelly: Good to see you, William. How are the passengers doing tonight?

William Goodwin: See for yourself. That's Frances Garner and her two boys, Samuel and Lewis. We've been on the water since sundown. We had to be careful, because the slave catchers are out tonight.

John Kelly: Yes, they are. We've been listening to their dogs for the last hour. I think they are on this side of the river, so we had better hurry.

William Goodwin: These folks are half-frozen.

Elias Kelly: Here, I brought some blankets.

John Kelly: Here you go, Mrs. Garner, wrap yourself and the boys in these. We've got no time to lose. The slave catchers are close by.

Samuel Garner: I'm cold, Mama. I can't even feel my fingers anymore.

Lewis Garner: Yes, and my feet are frozen.

Frances Garner: It's going to be alright, boys. These people will put us up for a while. We'll have a roof over our heads before too long.

Elias Kelly: There is a warm fire waiting for you, and a hot meal too. We've made up a nice bed so you can rest yourselves. We'll be home shortly.

John Kelly: William, why don't you come back with us and spend the night?

William Goodwin: No, but thanks for the offer. If I don't get home by midnight, my wife will get sick with worry. Now help me shove off.

(After pushing the boat back into the water, John and Elias gather up the family's meager belongings and escort Frances and her children away. The sound of the bloodhounds grows louder and more menacing.

When he is sure the others are safely on their way, William Goodwin pulls on his oars and heads back up the river.)

Scene 2

Inside the Cambridge Quaker Meeting House

Narrator: Frances Garner and her sons have found shelter in the Kelly home. They have come at a time when members of the Quaker community are divided over how to deal with runaway slaves. This topic is becoming increasingly important. More and more runaway slaves are coming to the Quakers for help getting to the North. When Quakers face a difficult issue, they may hold a meeting where everyone is free to express his or her views on the subject. It is hoped that by sharing different opinions, a new awareness or understanding will grow.

As the scene opens, the Cambridge Quaker members are holding a meeting about helping runaway slaves. John and Elizabeth Kelly are present, along with Elias, their oldest son.

Clerk of the Meeting: *(Sitting at a table, facing the members. Beside him sits the Meeting Secretary.)*

Friends, we are gathered today to consider a very urgent matter. As you know, our government has been making it increasingly difficult to help runaway slaves escape to the North. It is now considered a crime to help those who have escaped from bondage and travel north in search of freedom.

The question before us is this: How shall we continue to support our black brothers and sisters? Should we avoid doing anything that is illegal or likely to cause violence against us? Or should we refuse to obey this unjust law? In the spirit of worship, may we clearly see the way ahead.

Quaker Man 1: As long as there is slavery, nobody is free, black or white. If even one of us is in chains, we are all in chains.

Quaker Man 2: But what are we to do about slavery and the laws that allow it? I say it is time to take action. Let us begin by openly refusing to abide by this appalling law, no matter what the cost.

Quaker Man 1: I agree. We must take a stand when the laws are unjust.

Quaker Woman 1: I disagree. I am a widow with three children to care for. I am not willing to go to jail or pay a fine of several hundred dollars for breaking the law. Patience is what we need to practice. We should not disobey the law.

Elizabeth Kelly: Patience? We have been patient for far too long. While we are quietly being patient, our brothers and sisters in slave-owning states are living worse than dogs. I believe the only decent thing we can do is break the law.

Elias Kelly: My mother has already paid a price for her views. It is no secret that certain people have tried to discipline her for being outspoken. As a fellow Friend, I support my mother and all those who oppose by word and deed this dreadful law.

Quaker Woman 1: We all oppose the pro-slavery laws by word, but we shouldn't oppose them by deed.

Quaker Man 3: If young Elias Kelly and his mother have their way, we will likely have mobs of angry people storming our Meeting House. Like it or not, we must obey the law. To do otherwise is to invite chaos into our midst and prevent us from doing God's work.

Quaker Woman 2: As Friends, we do not support slavery and we do not keep slaves. That is enough.

Quaker Man 2: Slavery has existed in the United States since before the Revolution. That is far too long. It shouldn't have been tolerated then, and it should not be tolerated now.

Quaker Woman 3: Yes, people are kept like cattle and forced to work. Slavery is a crime against everything we stand for.

Quaker Man 3: I still don't think we should break the law.

John Kelly: Whatever we decide today will not stop the flood of fugitive slaves rising up from the South. When a runaway shows up on our doorstep, what are we to do? Turn him in because that is what the law demands? My conscience says no. Let us stand on the side of the slave, not the master!

(Elizabeth and Elias stand to show their support for John.)

Elias Kelly: *(Whispering)* Good work, Father.

(Some members stand in support of John Kelly's position, which has caused quite a disturbance in the usually peaceful Meeting House. Other members remain seated.)

Quaker Man 1: It seems we are undecided about this difficult issue.

Quaker Woman 1: Yes, we could go on discussing this all night. I need to get home and rest. We have much to decide.

Clerk of the Meeting: Friends, we are adjourned. Let the secretary note in the minutes that the group failed to achieve unity and that further discussion is needed.

Act II

The Setting

Cambridge, Maryland, April 1857

Scene 1

In the kitchen of the Kelly home

Narrator: Tensions continue to grow throughout Maryland as antislavery citizens step up their fight against slavery. Slave owners, on the other hand, struggle to protect their way of life and do whatever they can to keep runaways out of the state.

At the home of John and Elizabeth Kelly, the family of runaways has found shelter. By now, the Garners should have already moved on to the next station. But for the time being, they'll have to stay where they are. It's too risky to travel. Too many people are watching for runaways and for anyone who might be helping them. As the scene opens, Elizabeth Kelly and Frances Garner are having tea in the kitchen and mending clothes for their children. It is late in the afternoon on a cool day in early spring. As they sew, the women start to talk about why Frances decided to take her boys and leave the South for good.

Elizabeth Kelly: Frances, I must tell you that your sewing is lovely. Such straight stitches!

Frances Garner: Well, Mrs. Kelly, I've had time enough to learn my sewing. I did most of the sewing for the plantation owners.

Elizabeth Kelly: Well, you have a talent. It's all I can do to keep my stitches in line. Oh, I nearly forgot, would you care for some sweet-potato biscuits with your tea?

Frances Garner: Thank you, yes, ma'am. I'm mighty grateful for the food, but I'm worried. I haven't stayed in one place for so long since I took my boys and ran away as fast as our legs would carry us.

Elizabeth Kelly: Rest assured, Frances, you can stay with us as long as you need to.

Frances Garner: My boys like it here, that's for sure. But we've got a long way to go before we can call a place home. We need to go where I can work and get a place where the three of us can live. They tell me Canada is the area to head for.

Elizabeth Kelly: I don't mean to pry, but what made you decide to come north? We don't have to talk about it if you don't want to.

Frances Garner: Well, since I was a little girl, I tried to imagine what the word *freedom* meant. I heard it time and time again, but for the life of me I didn't know what it meant. Then one day I understood. It was the morning they took my husband away and sold him to some family in Mississippi.

Elizabeth Kelly: But how could they do such a thing? What reason could there be?

Frances Garner: There was a bad harvest, and the plantation owner needed the money.

Elizabeth Kelly: So he sold your husband?

Frances Garner: Yes, and others, too. Mine wasn't the only family that was broken apart.

Elizabeth Kelly: I suppose there was nothing you could do to stop them.

Frances Garner: That's right, ma'am. Nothing I could do except scream and kick and claw. It took three men to hold me back while I watched my husband being dragged off in chains and flung into the back of a wagon like he was no better than a bale of cotton.

Elizabeth Kelly: I'm so sorry, Frances.

Frances Garner: I understood then and there that freedom was something I had to get for my boys and myself, or my heart would shrivel up and die like an old, brown leaf in winter.

Elizabeth Kelly: You are a brave woman, Frances.

(Martha Purvis, a free black woman who works on the Kelly farm, rushes in frantically. She is out of breath and very upset.)

Elizabeth Kelly: *(Startled)* Good gracious, Martha! Why, you nearly scared me half to death! I thought you were a slave catcher and that we were done for.

Martha Purvis: I'm sorry to have frightened you, but please, I need your help! You must come right now!

Elizabeth Kelly: Of course! Tell me what's wrong. Why are you shaking?

(Elias, James, and Hannah, startled by the commotion, enter the kitchen, eager to find out what's going on.)

Martha Purvis: It's my husband. They just locked him up. The sheriff said he robbed somebody and stabbed him, which he never would do. Never! He's a good man, an honest man. Besides, I know where my husband was when that fellow got robbed. He was in the back of our own house, fixing the chicken coop.

Elizabeth Kelly: Here, sit down and try to calm yourself, Martha. It won't do any good to get frantic.

Martha Purvis: I can't help it. A bunch of white men want to break him out and **lynch** him. They say that'll show runaways what'll happen to them if they pass through Maryland.

Elizabeth Kelly: But your husband isn't a slave. He's a free man!

Martha Purvis: That doesn't make any difference. We've got the wrong skin color. I'm sorry to bother you, but I didn't know where else to go. Folks in this town, they respect you and your husband. They'll listen to what you have to say. But you have to come now, before it's too late!

Elizabeth Kelly: We'll do what we can, Martha. I'll look for John. He's most likely in the barn. We'll take the wagon into town as long as the roads are clear.

(Elias steps towards his mother and Martha.)

Elias Kelly: James and I are going with you, Mother.

Hannah Kelly: So am I.

Elizabeth Kelly: Very well. But stay together. There's no telling what a mob of angry people will do. They may even turn on us. Frances, please be extra careful while we are away.

---

lynch – to kill for a crime without a lawful trial

Elias Kelly: I'll go and hitch the wagon. Hannah, I'll need help with the horses.

Scene 2

In front of the jail in town

Narrator: The Kelly family, along with Martha Purvis, travel by wagon into town hoping they can stop an angry mob of pro-slavery citizens from lynching Martha's husband. As the scene opens, a crowd of men have surrounded the Cambridge town jail. Some of the men are carrying guns. One man, sitting loftily on his horse, holds a rope in his hand. He appears to be the ringleader. A couple of his accomplices are dragging Frederick Purvis toward the street. The sheriff, who has been roughed up by the men, staggers out of the jail.

Sheriff Hollings: Let Purvis go! I'm the law here!

Ned Delaney: Wrong, Sheriff. Today we're the law, and we've got a sentence to carry out. Right, men?

(The men raise their rifles and loudly cheer in response to Delaney's question.)

Ned Delaney: This thief is going to hang for sure.

Sheriff Hollings: You're making a big mistake, Delaney. You're taking the law into your own hands. You'll be committing a terrible crime. Now you let him go!

(Delaney signals the men who are standing close to the sheriff. The men grab the sheriff from behind and bind his hands with a rope.)

Ned Delaney: *(To the men holding Frederick Purvis)* Tie him up. We'll take him over to the town square where the whole town can watch him swing.

(The Kelly family and Martha Purvis arrive.)

John Kelly: I think you better untie Purvis and let him be on his way.

Ned Delaney: Stay out of this, John Kelly.

John Kelly: Frederick Purvis works on my farm. He's a good man. A hardworking man. A man who loves his family, same as the rest of us. And he's a man who's part of this town, same as you and me.

Ned Delaney: Black folks have to learn their place. We got too many of them thinking they're just as good as white folks, and too many runaways coming through here **inciting** our slaves to think about leaving. We're going to put a stop to that.

---

incite – to move into action; stir up

John Kelly: You think that by hanging Frederick Purvis you're going to stop what's happening in Maryland and the whole country? If you honestly believe that, Ned Delaney, then you're a bigger fool than I thought.

Ned Delaney: *(Pointing his gun at John Kelly)* I think we're done talking. *(To his men)* Put the noose around his neck.

(Martha runs to her husband's side. John Kelly steps between Purvis and Delaney.)

John Kelly: Purvis stays here. I will not let you harm a man who has done no wrong.

(John's wife and children stand beside him.)

Ned Delaney: Step away, John Kelly. I don't want to hurt you or your family. Go home.

Elizabeth Kelly: No, Mr. Delaney. This is our town, too, and we're not going to stand by and let you murder one of our own. Fred Purvis is a free man, not a slave. He deserves a fair trial, like any other man.

Hannah Kelly: Sir, your son Tom and I have been friends since we were six years old. We learned to read together. Last summer, my brother James helped you patch up the well on your farm. Do you remember?

James Kelly: And when one of your cows was nearly dying, Frederick Purvis saved her and her calf.

John Kelly: This is his home as much as yours or mine, Ned Delaney. You have no right to hurt him. He never caused you any harm. And that goes for you others, too. John Osborne, I see you in the crowd. Didn't Fred Purvis mend your fences last spring? Didn't you tell me that he did good work and gave you a good price? And you, Virgil Tibbs. Didn't Purvis fix your mother's roof while you were away last winter? I don't believe he even charged you for the work. Folks, this man deserves a fair hearing. Is there any evidence that he even committed this crime?

(People in the crowd are beginning to look uncomfortable. Many are nodding in agreement with John Kelly. Ned Delaney keeps his gun raised and pointed at John Kelly, but it's clear that he's backing down. After a very tense silence, Delaney finally puts down his gun.)

Ned Delaney: *(To the men still holding Frederick Purvis)* Let him go. *(To John Kelly)* It's not over, Kelly, not by a long shot. I know people like you are helping runaways. We'll catch you yet. And then we'll see if your powerful speeches will help you.

(Delaney picks up the reins of his horse and rides away. The lynch mob goes home. Martha Purvis unties her husband's hands. John Kelly embraces his wife and children.)

Elias Kelly: I've never been so frightened in all my life.

John Kelly: I know how you feel, son.

Elias Kelly: You do? But the way you held your ground and looked Ned Delaney right in the eye—I never knew anyone could be that brave.

Hannah Kelly: Maybe the secret of courage is to not let your fear get the upper hand.

James Kelly: I don't know about the secret of courage, but I do know that I'm tired. Can we go home now?

Scene 3

In the living room of the Kelly home

Narrator: Elias Kelly, who is out of school and working as an apprentice at the local newspaper, hopes to be a writer one day. After seeing how his father was able to talk Ned Dclaney out of lynching Frederick Purvis, young Elias decides to write an article about what happened. The editor of the paper likes the article and prints it in the next edition of the paper. As the scene opens, Elias has just pointed out his article to John Kelly, who has begun to read what his son has written. Elias eagerly awaits his father's reaction.

John Kelly: *(Reading)* "John Kelly, a local farmer, recently put his principles to the test. Staring down the barrel of a gun, Mr. Kelly defended the life of Frederick Purvis, a black man who had been dragged from his jail cell and threatened with lynching by a mob of pro-slavery citizens. . . ."

(Putting down the newspaper) Elias, how could you write such a thing?

Elias Kelly: But, Father, I thought you would be pleased. All I did was tell the truth.

John Kelly: There is a time and a place for everything. We need to promote unity, not divide people. This dear country of ours is splitting in two. Your article will only make matters worse by inflaming tempers on both sides of the issue.

Elias Kelly: I don't agree. People have to hear the truth. Those who believe that slavery and the enforcement of an unjust law are wrong must have examples by which to live. What you did the other night is such an example. It will inspire others, as it has inspired me.

(Someone shouts from the front yard.)

Ned Delaney: John Kelly, show your face!

John Kelly: Elias, where are Frances and the children?

Elias Kelly: In the barn with Mother. They wanted to get out of the house for a while.

John Kelly: Sneak out the back door and tell your mother to hide them in the hayloft. They are not to make a sound. Do you hear me? Not a sound!

(As Elias sneaks out the back door in the kitchen, John Kelly opens the front door and steps outside. He sees Ned Delaney standing with a couple of armed men.)

Ned Delaney: I read your son's article in the paper. So did a lot of folks. Some of them are here with me today, and I have to tell you, Kelly, we're not happy. Elias called us "a venomous mob of hateful men intent on taking the law into their own hands and lynching an innocent black man." He went on to say that those who own slaves or believe in the institution of slavery are no better than barbarians.

John Kelly: He's still young. He has a lot to learn. I'm sorry if his words caused you folks any distress. Now I've got chores that need doing. I have nothing else to say to you.

(John Kelly turns and begins to walk back up the path leading to his house.)

Ned Delaney: Don't turn your back on me! I have every reason to believe you're hiding a bunch of runaways. You and your boy have accused me of taking the law into my own hands. It appears to me, Kelly, that the only lawbreaker around here is you.

(He takes out a silver badge and flashes it toward John Kelly.)

You know what this is? It's a badge. That's right, a badge. Sheriff Hollings made me one of his deputies. That means, as a sworn upholder of the law, I am

obliged to search your house for fugitives. Let's
go, men.

*(Ned Delaney leads his men across the front yard and
up the steps of the house. Once again, John Kelly
stands his ground.)*

John Kelly: This is my home, and I will not permit you
to enter it.

*(Ned Delaney signals to his men. Without warning,
they charge at John Kelly, knocking him down.)*

Ned Delaney: *(To his men)* There are runaways here.
I know it. We'll find them even if we have to burn
this place to the ground.

(They go inside the house.)

Scene 4
Outside the Kelly barn

Narrator: Ned Delaney came to the home of the Kelly
family, planning to get even for what happened outside
the city jail. He also wanted to look for runaways. He
was sure John and Elizabeth were hiding slaves
somewhere on their property. After searching the
house and finding nothing, Delaney and his men went

to the barn. They set it on fire as a warning to the Kelly family to stop standing up for blacks, free or enslaved. Thanks to the quick thinking of Elias Kelly, Frances Garner and her children were unharmed. In the nick of time, he smuggled them out of the barn and into the root cellar. Ned Delaney searched the house but did not find the cellar. The scene opens as the family is inspecting the smoldering ruins of their barn.

James Kelly: What a mess! What are we going to do now?

John Kelly: We will have to rebuild. Barns can be replaced. Let us be thankful that the barn was the only thing destroyed.

Elizabeth Kelly: John, how is your head? Let me look at that cut. I still can't believe those men attacked you!

John Kelly: I wish I could be as surprised as you are. Ned Delaney uses violence to prove he is right to himself and to others. And we are standing in his way.

Elizabeth Kelly: Yes, he's made it clear that he wants to punish poor Frances, and anyone who will help her.

John Kelly: We can't put our own family in danger. Maybe there are other things we can do to help runaway slaves, just as the Friends were saying.

Hannah Kelly: No, Father, we are not going to give up, and we're not going to turn in Frances and her children. You taught us that we must help protect those who cannot protect themselves.

John Kelly: Children, look around you. The men who did this are dead-set on stopping us and everyone else who believes the way we do. The next time it could be our home or one of us. I can't let that happen.

Elizabeth Kelly: We always knew sooner or later things would turn violent. Now they have. They mean to scare us and they've succeeded. But we're not alone, John. We're part of something that's as deep and wide as a river.

Elias Kelly: Father, you raised me to put my trust in things I can't see with my eyes or touch with my hands. Isn't this one of those times when people have to fall back on that kind of trust? We have to go forward with our work despite these obstacles.

John Kelly: I don't know, son. I see the remains of our barn. I smell the smoke from the fire. I recall the look of hatred in Ned Delaney's eyes. I know these things to be true. But what we should do now—that's something I just don't know.

Hannah Kelly: What about Frances and her children? They're counting on us. We have to think about them, too. We're doing all this to help them escape.

Elias Kelly: One thing is certain. We can't let them stay here any longer. We've got to at least get them out of the county, if not the state.

Hannah Kelly: The sooner the better, I say. We can only hope there are fewer people like Ned Delaney wherever the Garners must go.

Elizabeth Kelly: Rebecca Hadley and some other ladies told me the other day that there are a lot of runaways in the county, which means there's probably a lot of slave catchers looking for them.

John Kelly: That's what I'm so worried about. With so many slave catchers around and half the town up in arms against people like us, all the conductors are lying low, waiting for the right moment to get things moving again.

Elizabeth Kelly: All I'm saying is that maybe we'll just have to let Frances stay with us a while longer.

Elias Kelly: I don't agree, Mother. We can't let her stay here. It's too dangerous—for us and for her.

Hannah Kelly: I agree with Elias. We've helped other people find their way to freedom, but it's never been as dangerous as it is right now. We have to find a way to help the Garners, and waiting will make things worse.

John Kelly: They're right, Elizabeth. If Frances or her boys are hurt or killed, it would be a terrible tragedy. If something bad happens to one of us, we may not be able to help the Garners escape. We could go to jail and I don't even want to think about what might happen to Frances and her boys. We just can't take that risk. It's too dangerous.

Elizabeth Kelly: But if everyone is watching, how can we let her go? If they catch her, it could be the end of her family.

James Kelly: That's what I'm trying to figure out. I just don't see a way that we can get Frances out of here without anybody knowing about it.

Hannah Kelly: Maybe we should ask the Friends to help us decide what to do.

James Kelly: I like that idea. We can't figure this out all by ourselves. We need other Friends.

Elias Kelly: James, that's the smartest thing I've heard you say in a long time.

John Kelly: Then it's settled. We'll take our concern to our fellow Friends and pray we can find the strength to keep doing what's right.

Act III

The Setting

Cambridge, Maryland, May 1857

Scene 1

Inside the Cambridge Quaker Meeting House

Narrator: John Kelly has asked the Clerk to call a special meeting. The Clerk agreed. The following Sunday, the Friends meet to decide on a clear course of action. The community is facing a crisis, and something needs to be done.

Clerk of the Meeting: Friends, the last few weeks have seen an upsurge in violent actions against those who stand for the equality of all men.

Hannah Kelly: And all women, too.

Clerk of the Meeting: And all women, too. As most of you know, there are many runaways among us. Like hornets around the hive, slave catchers are swarming around our town. The question before us is this: Should we obey the law and not help runaway slaves, or should we help slaves escape to freedom?

Quaker Woman 1: My sister is a Friend in Phillips County. She told me in a letter that some men threatened to burn down the Meeting House. They said the Friends were hiding fugitives on the premises, and some of the members were hiding them in their homes. I ask all of you who are helping runaways to think of the danger you are putting us in. You should find some other way to express your beliefs.

Quaker Man 1: Rachel, I must remind you that those are beliefs we all share. The fugitives in our midst are our responsibility. We cannot turn our backs on them. We're all they have.

Quaker Woman 2: Do not forget, Friends, that while we are sitting here, our black brothers and sisters throughout the South are being sold like cattle to the highest bidder. It is our duty to do whatever we can to end this evil once and for all.

Martha Purvis: My husband and I came to Maryland from out of town a while back. We could've taken our kids and kept on going, but we stayed. We found what we were looking for right here in this county. We found it in the hands of Friends much like yourselves. Now we belong to this group and draw strength from it. I see what has to be done, and I call on all of you to find the courage to do it.

Quaker Man 1: Friends, it occurs to me that the Baltimore Yearly Meeting will be in session next week. I propose that we form a committee that will travel there to discuss this issue with our fellow Friends.

Quaker Man 2: Perhaps those who are able to attend the Yearly Meeting might form a kind of caravan with wagons and carriages.

Quaker Woman 2: I hear that a good many poor people in Baltimore are suffering hard times and need all the help they can get. We will have to bring them many provisions and supplies.

Hannah Kelly: We could load the wagons with provisions and then hide Frances and her sons in one of the wagons.

James Kelly: But what if the slave catchers get suspicious and decide to search the wagons?

Elizabeth Kelly: We'll divide the caravan in two. Most of the wagons will travel north to Baltimore. The rest, maybe two or three, will take the road west. It will take longer, but they can meet up with the main wagons close to Baltimore.

John Kelly: I agree with my wife. It's our best chance of getting Frances and her sons out of Maryland. We will make sure that the people in the town know we are making the journey and when we are leaving. The wagons with the runaways can leave earlier. This way they are sure to avoid Delaney and his men.

Clerk of the Meeting: Are we all in agreement with the proposal put forward by our members?

(Members raise their hands or say, "Aye," to express their agreement. It is unanimous.)

Let it be noted that today, May 5, 1857, the Cambridge Friends resolved to travel in caravan style to the Baltimore Yearly Meeting.

Scene 2

Outside the Kelly home

Narrator: John and Elizabeth Kelly left the meeting feeling very proud of their daughter's bold idea. With little time to waste, the family returned home and sat down with Frances Garner and her two children. They told the fugitives about the plan that had been discussed at the meeting. As the scene opens just before sunrise, the Kelly family is preparing for the long journey to Baltimore. Elias Kelly is busy hitching the horses to the family wagon. Two other wagons are lined up on the road in front of the house.

Elizabeth Kelly: Hannah and I baked some pies for you and the children.

Frances Garner: That's very nice of you, Mrs. Kelly. We appreciate all your kindness. But I was wondering if you could answer a question for me. If you don't mind my asking, what's this Yearly Meeting you have been talking about?

Hannah Kelly: It's when all of the Quakers in the surrounding area get together. We do this once a year. That's why we call it the Yearly Meeting.

Elizabeth Kelly: When you get to Baltimore, people there will look after you, Frances. If things go according to plan, you might just make it to Canada by summer.

Hannah Kelly: *(To Samuel and Lewis Garner)* You can have this book if you like. *(She gives them the book of stories she's been reading aloud to them.)* I'm sure one day real soon you boys will learn to read. I bet you'll even write stories of your own.

Samuel Garner: When I do, I'll write you a long letter, Hannah. I'll tell you all about our new home.

Lewis Garner: Me, too.

Quaker Man 1: Everything's set now. Are you folks ready to get going?

John Kelly: We're about as ready as we'll ever be. Mrs. Garner, you and your boys will ride in this man's wagon. His name is Joseph Hollins. We'll meet up with you later on.

Frances Garner: *(Taking Elizabeth's hand one last time)* Goodbye, dear woman. Thank you for your kindness. Thank you all. I won't ever forget what you have done for my boys and me. *(The Quaker man escorts her to his wagon.)* Come on, boys. Time to go. *(Samuel and Lewis follow her.)*

Quaker Man 1: I made a little nest in the hay for you and the boys, Mrs. Garner, right behind the fruit baskets. I put some blankets in there, too. It'll be cramped, but there's no other way. No telling who's around, keeping an eye on things. Let's pray they haven't figured out we are taking a different road.

John Kelly: Elias, have you finished with the horses?

Elias Kelly: Yes, Father.

James Kelly: Can I come, too?

Elizabeth Kelly: No, James. You and Hannah have school to attend. *(To her husband)* Promise me you'll be careful, John. I don't want anything to happen to Frances or those two little boys. Where are you meeting up with Mr. Hollins's wagon?

John Kelly: Crawford's Notch. It should be quite a gathering. I figure at least 12 wagons in all. With any luck, Delaney will fall right into our trap and stop Elias and me before we get there.

Elizabeth Kelly: You two be careful. Delaney won't give up until he's found what he's looking for.

(John Kelly releases the brake on the wagon wheels and gives the reins a jolt.)

Scene 3

A country road outside Cambridge

Narrator: John and Elias Kelly head north for Baltimore, about sixty miles away. The other two wagons head west, with Frances Garner and her sons tucked away in the back of one of them. Later that morning, Ned Delaney and his men ride up behind the main wagon train and order the drivers to stop. As the scene opens, Delaney is searching the wagons. The Kelly wagon is next.

Ned Delaney: Looks like we meet again, Kelly.

John Kelly: We're not doing anything wrong. You have no right to stop our wagons.

Ned Delaney: You see this gun in my hand? It gives me all the right I need. Now if you don't want me to use it, I suggest you get down off your wagon and stand on the other side of the road like the rest of the drivers. I know who you're trying to hide, and I intend to find them. Now get down off the wagon.

Elias Kelly: You're wasting your time, Delaney. We're only bringing some food and blankets to poor folks up in Baltimore, just like the rest of the wagons here.

Ned Delaney: That's not what I heard. I heard you Quakers are **smuggling** runaways. I'm a lawman now, and I've got a job to do, which is to catch fugitives and turn them over to their proper owners. That's the law, whether you like it or not.

John Kelly: That law is totally unjust. Any man who attempts to enforce it is breaking a higher law.

Elias Kelly: Father, maybe we should just do what Mr. Delaney wants us to do.

Ned Delaney: Listen to your son, Kelly. He's no fool. I don't want to have to hurt you.

John Kelly: You burned down my barn, you threatened my family, and now you point a gun at me and say you'll shoot me in cold blood if I don't do what you want. That's a whole lot of hurt right there, Delaney.

Elias Kelly: Please, Father, hold your temper.

John Kelly: You want to search my wagon, Delaney? Go ahead. But I'm not stepping down.

Ned Delaney: Rip it open, boys! I know he's got runaways in there. No doubt about it. I'll catch them if it's the last thing I do.

---

smuggle – to secretly or illegally move something or someone from one place to another

Narrator: Ned Delaney and his men searched every nook and cranny in the back of John Kelly's wagon. All they found were baskets of apples, sweet potatoes, and turnips. Two smoked hams, some salted fish and chests full of used clothes. By the time they finished their search, the wagon carrying Frances Garner and her sons was safely on its way to Baltimore and freedom.

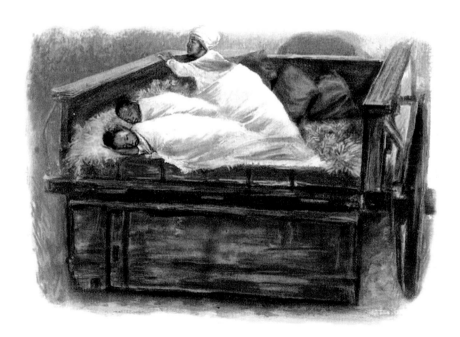

Epilogue

Narrator: After helping the Garner family escape safely from Maryland, John Kelly and his family continued to help other runaway slaves. Ned Delaney and others continued to pressure those who were against slavery, making work on the Underground Railroad more and more dangerous. Tension in the community continued to grow, much as it did across the country. But the Kelly family did not waver. They continued helping runaway slaves until the Civil War broke out in 1861.

Frances Garner and her two sons escaped from Maryland unharmed. Frances had her heart set on bringing her family to Canada, but, after traveling the Underground Railroad for three more months, she decided to settle in Albany, New York. In Albany, the Garners stayed with a family Frances met through a local church. When Frances found a job as a seamstress, she was finally able to rent a small house for herself and her sons. Life was hard, but each day Frances knew she had finally found the meaning of freedom.

Slavery and Freedom in America

The Underground Railroad

Many slaves ran away from their owners. They headed for states in the North where slavery was not allowed. They also headed for Canada. Many escaped slaves traveled along the Underground Railroad. The Underground Railroad was not actually a railroad. It was a system of routes that led from southern slave states to the North.

A safe place where runaways could rest and get food was called a station. People who helped runaway slaves were called conductors. One very famous conductor on the Underground Railroad was a former slave named Harriet Tubman.

This Underground Railroad station had a secret room, hidden behind shelves.

The Quakers

Quakers are a Christian group also known as the Religious Society of Friends. Quakers believe in peace, and condemn violence of any kind. They believe in equality for all, regardless of gender or race. In the 1800s, Quakers became leaders in the antislavery movement. Many Quakers helped runaway slaves escape to the North.

Quaker Anthony Benezet teaching slave children to read

The Civil War

By the late 1850s, slavery had divided the United States. The North wanted to abolish slavery. The South wanted it to remain. During the 1860 presidential campaign, Abraham Lincoln said he wanted to stop the spread of slavery. This angered many Southerners. When Lincoln became president, southern states began to leave the United States to form their own country. They called themselves The Confederate States of America. In 1861, war broke out between the North and the South. The Civil War lasted for four long years. Many people were killed on both sides. On April 9, 1865, the South surrendered to the North. The United States remained one country. Slavery was abolished, and all former slaves were set free.

President Abraham Lincoln

❧ Read, Research, and Write ❧

Write a Newspaper Article

Imagine the year is 1857. You are a reporter assigned to explain the different opinions on slavery in Cambridge, Maryland.

- Copy the chart shown below into your notebook.

- In the left column, list three events discussed in the story that show different opinions, in the order they occurred.

- In the second column, list information about each event.

- Use the information from the story and other resources to complete your chart.

- Then write your article. Use dates and clue words such as *first, next, then,* and *last* to show the sequence of the events.

Events	Information about the event
1. There are different opinions on helping slaves among members of the Quaker community.	Quakers believe that slavery is wrong. Some Quakers want to obey the Fugitive Slave Act.
2.	
3.	

Read More About the Underground Railroad

Find and read more books about the Underground Railroad. As you read, think about these questions. They will help you understand more about this topic.

- Why was being a conductor along the Underground Railroad risky?

- Why didn't more slaves use the Underground Railroad?

- What challenges did freed slaves face after completing their journey on the Underground Railroad?

- What are some other ways people helped end slavery in the 1800s?

SUGGESTED READING
Reading Expeditions
People Who Changed America:
The Anti-Slavery Movement